STONES

from the

MUSE

Runes *for the*
Creative Journey

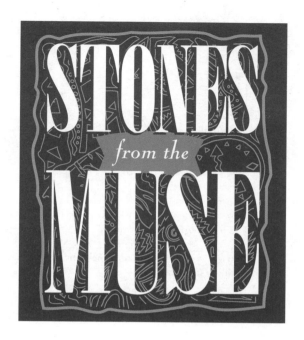

Runes *for the* Creative Journey

by Emily Herman & Jennifer Richard Jacobson

A Fireside Book

Published by Simon & Schuster

FIRESIDE
Rockefeller Center
1230 Avenue of the Americas
New York, New York 10020

Stones from the Muse is produced by becker&mayer!, Ltd. From
Stones from the Muse packaged set, which includes ten two-sided
runes, a cloth storage bag, and this book.

Designed by Sullivan Scully Design Group
Art direction by Simon Sung
Edited by Alison Herschberg
Book printed in China. Packaging manufactured in China.
Components manufactured in China.

10 9 8 7 6 5 4 3 2 1

Library of Congress Cataloging-in-Publication
data is available.

ISBN 0-684-83955-5

CONTENTS

. . . .

LIST of RUNES

WINDOW
Vision—By throwing open the shutters, we grow in perception or acquire a view.

Where there is no vision, the people perish.
— Proverb

. . . .

SEED
Ideas—Ideas, like seeds, will grow only if they land in fertile, well-tended soil.

The seed of the idea is developed by both labor and the unconscious, and the struggle that goes on between them.
— Carson McCullers

. . . .

MASK
Fear—Artists have the tools to pass through the natural blocks fear builds as they struggle to create.

I had to get over my fear of running through the world naked and learn to say, "Take me or leave me."
— Steven Spielberg

KNAPSACK
Play—Some artistic work can only be accomplished through play.

Play is the exultation of the possible.
— Martin Buber

. . . .

TOOL
Action—Taking action is the way a creative piece moves from ephemeral dreams to solid reality.

Never retract, never explain, never apologize…get the thing done and let them howl.
—Nellie McClery

. . . .

WHIRLWIND
Chaos—It is through the acceptance of chaos and the discovery of patterns within that creative work can be done.

Sell your cleverness and buy bewilderment.
—Jalal ud-Din Rumi

GAVEL
Judgment—Critics, both within and without, come dressed in many different costumes, and it is the artist's work to decide when and to whom to listen.

It is not easy to find happiness in ourselves, and it is not possible to find it elsewhere.
—Agnes Repplier

. . . .

CLOCK
Organization—Structure, rather than being tyrannical to the creative soul, can offer freedom essential for an artistic life.

You've got to own your days and name them, each one of them, or else the years go right by and none of them belong to you.
—Herb Gardner

. . . .

ARROW
Vulnerability—An artist with a new vision to share has every reason to feel vulnerable.

I get up, I walk, I fall down. Meanwhile I keep dancing.

—Rabbi Hillel

X
Failure—By accepting failure artists can move on.

Give me a fruitful error anytime, full of seeds, bursting with its own corrections.
—Vilfredo Pareto

LIST of RUNES

EGG
Potential—The life of an artist is the tension between what is and what could be.

The difference between the right word and the almost right word is the difference between lightning and the lightning bug.
  —Mark Twain

. . . .

[BLANK]
Silence—Silence, a most essential tool, allows the space necessary for creativity to occur.

Silence is the mother of truth.
  —Benjamin Disraeli

. . . .

MOON
Dream Time—Honor your dreams—even if they are nightmares— not as lessons or answers, but as scents to flavor your life and your work.

We are such stuff as dreams are made on, and our little life is rounded with a sleep.
  —William Shakespeare

AMULET
Honor—It is time to acknowledge and trust your unique instincts.

This is my place to stand.
  —Maori saying

. . . .

SCALE
Balance—Developing a creative piece—as well as living an artistic life—requires a balancing act.

There is a time for work. And a time for love. That leaves no other time.
  —Coco Chanel

. . . .

TADPOLE
Transformation—By recognizing change in our art, we transform ourselves.

The future enters into us, in order to transform itself in us, long before it happens.
  —Rainer Maria Rilke

CUP
Recharge—Take a break from the intensity of creating; who knows what you'll discover when you return?

I can always be distracted by love, but eventually I get horny for my creativity.
—Gilda Radner

. . . .

LENS
Revision—In the process of fleshing out a vision, an artist often shifts away from the original premise; through revision, the amount and value of this shift can be recognized.

A piece of sculpture or a painting is never a finished work. Simultaneously it answers a question which has been asked, and asks a new question.
—Robert Engman

RIBBON
Celebration—Throughout the creative process there are moments that deserve celebration; it is in the artist's best interest to find these moments and to celebrate to the fullest.

Surely the strange beauty of the world must somewhere rest on pure joy.
—Louise Bogan

. . . .

GATE
Marketing—It's time to toot your own horn! Share your work with confidence, know-how, and a dose of detachment.

If one advances in the direction of his dreams, one will meet success unexpected in common hours.
—Henry David Thoreau

Stones *from the* Muse
Runes *for the* Creative Journey

. . . .

INTRODUCTION

Artists are a superstitious lot. We have to be. We perform magic using everyday materials—words, sounds, clay, color, perspective, movements. We create characters, moods—even worlds—by putting these materials together.

But we know the process of creating is anything but simple. There are inexplicable blank spots when sounds don't come; when shapes remain lifeless; when words dissolve into meaningless drivel. And even when the act of creating flows smoothly, problems with marketing can keep artists from sharing their work. Artists use different media; their daily habits are dissimilar; but all artists, at different times, find themselves in various stages of a creative process. Most develop patterns or rituals to help them deal with artistic uncertainties, to say nothing of the vagaries of the world. But we often need more—direction and wisdom as certain (and uniquely our own) as a stone thrown through the window of our garret, with a message directly from our muse.

So here are some stones from the muse. Instead of coming through the window, these stones are drawn from a bag. Each is marked with two symbols—one on each side. Each symbol offers direction, guidance, and sometimes a gentle shove off the edge of a cliff. Pull a stone out of the bag, and place it in front of you. Examine the symbol, read the commentary and think about it, and then get back to work. You'll know what you need to do.

How *to* Use These Stones

. . . .

The simplest way to use these stones to guide you in your creative work is to draw one from the bag each morning when you first wake. Hold the stone and hold yourself still. Now, without looking, without thinking, place the stone in front of you. Examine the symbol that faces you. What does that symbol mean to you?

After you have listened to your own thoughts about this particular message from the muse, read the commentary. Think about how your thoughts blend with the commentary; notice any insights or apparent contradictions, and allow them to inform your creative process or project. Certain symbols will develop special meaning to you or the particular work you do. At the end of this book, there are pages for personal notes. If you jot down ideas or the consequences of responding to a particular rune in a certain way, the runes will better feed your particular creative process.

Sometimes you will have a question about your work. It might be as specific as "How do I complete this piece?" or as general as "What will today be like?" In either case, hold the question in your mind as you draw a stone from your muse.

You might use a stone you draw from the bag in the morning as a starting point to get your work flowing. Or you may want to meditate on the meaning behind a stone's symbol and how it relates to an ongoing project. On some overwhelming days, you may need to keep a stone in your pocket; by touching it now and then, you'll remember you are an artist even if at this moment you can't be working.

Feel free to draw more than one stone during the day. Whenever you feel blocked or disoriented, pull a stone out of the bag and think about what it means to you.

There are times when your work needs to be placed in perspective. For this, it helps to draw three or four stones. The first might indicate past actions; the second, present considerations; the third, future actions; if you choose a fourth, it might suggest goals or results. Be sure to replace each stone in the bag before you choose again. Every symbol must be available for each drawing.

These are the stones from your muse. Design your own rituals or system of readings—after all, you are a creative person, and it is crucial that these stones hold meaning for you. Make a pattern of stones such as a circle, triangle, or cross. Determine the meanings of the placements of the stones, or the *signifiers.* Sample signifiers may be *starting point, challenge, block, inspiration, mentor, completion, overall tone.* You can develop your own as well.

Just as in the layout of tarot cards, signifiers represent certain points in the layout of the runes. The purpose of the signifiers is to focus your thoughts and explorations on a particular aspect of your work. If you draw **Play** and place it in the position you determined would be your "starting point," you might think about beginning a new piece in a playful manner, whereas if you had drawn **Marketing**, your approach would be entirely different. If **Play** were placed in the position of *overall tone,* your sense and direction of the work would be different still. Each new stone you draw can add complexity and depth to contemplations of your artistic endeavors.

The following are some sample layouts. As you work with your stones, you may discover different issues you wish to explore. Feel free to design your own layouts based upon combinations of issues that are important to you. Configurations might include natural shapes (tree with root, trunk, crown, etc.); geometric shapes; or patterns based on time (human, solar, or lunar). Following are some sample configurations:

Configurations

. . . .

past *present* *future*

---

immediate picture *big picture*

action required

conscious

unconscious

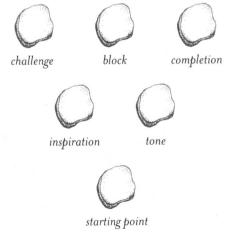

challenge   *block*   *completion*

inspiration   *tone*

starting point

past actions   *present considerations*   *future actions*   *goals/results*

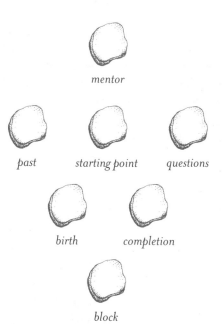

mentor

past   *starting point*   *questions*

birth   *completion*

block

WINDOW
Vision

. . . .

The window in your studio, the window to your mind, the window of your soul. Windows have always been the metaphor for *illumination* and a glimpse into the previously unknown.

Artists know the value of illumination. We throw open the shutters in an attempt to establish a vision, grow in perception, or acquire a view. We welcome the light—particularly in the form of a lightbulb over our heads.

Drawing this rune may foretell a time of inspiration. Open your mind to new possibilities. Look out a window—or *in* a window—for images. What shows on the bright surface? What lies in the shadows? Foreground? Background? Be reminded of messages in images and of their potential. As you look and listen, ask yourself: "How do I frame my vision? Could I look at this another way?" Perhaps a frame of a different size, shape, or material is in order.

Sometimes, however, light reveals nothing more than dust. If this is the case, close the curtains and revel in the dark for a while. Let faint wisps of ideas gently drift and curl inside you. Trust the darkness. Remain open and accepting during this period of incubation, and once again new insights will work their way to the light.

Keep in mind that visions, like the birds on the wire outside your window, are fleeting. Do pay attention.

FOR WINDOW, TRY THIS:

- What do you see through a window? Describe or sketch the view in a free-flowing manner. Make connections. Question the image. What does this picture mean to you?

- Shape an image in a medium different from your own. If you paint, try writing about the image. If you write, try composing a tune. If you compose, sculpt the image in available materials. Then bring the experience back to your art.

- Change the light you work by: dawn to dusk, artificial to natural; bulb to candle.

- Keep an inspiration box. Collect images: photographs, magazine pictures, newspaper clippings. Collect meaningful objects. Write down words that have power. Record your dreams. Store these together in your box. From time to time, empty the contents. Do you see any patterns? What if you put two unlike things together? Place the objects in different arrangements, and see what happens.

- Consider your future vision. Write three goals.

SEED
Ideas

. . . .

Your mind is like a compost heap. Stuff gets thrown in all the time—leftovers, garbage, fertilizer, earth. Fresh stuff, too. Living creatures make a home in the compost and burrow through it, turning and enriching it. The rain falls on it, moistening it. The sun warms it. And slowly, slowly, the compost pile develops its own heat. It steams. Recognizable chunks crumble. Soon this heap of waste becomes a fertile bed for new life. When a seed falls into a well-tended compost pile, it will flourish.

Ideas, like seeds, are everywhere. They fall into your mind at an incomprehensible rate. Some, not quite ripe, may themselves add to the compost. Others, finding the nutrients they need, will take root and grow. If you are feeling bereft of ideas, it is not because they aren't around you, but because you have some compost heap tending to do. This rune offers you the opportunity to roll up your sleeves and get to work. Pay attention to the fertility of your mind, the rich tidbits as well as the poisons you put in, and the time you give to feeding it. Too much garbage thrown in at once will pack down into a slimy, impenetrable mass. And compost heaps do have to be turned—not constantly, but now and then—to keep from becoming stagnant.

Ideas are everywhere, but not every idea can grow into a finished piece. As artist-gardener, you must do more than tend the compost heap: You must make choices. Which ideas are suited to your personality, your media, and which belong in someone else's garden?

Ideas will grow into lush works if honored and celebrated—and if they fall on fertile soil.

For Seed, Try This:

- Draw a picture of the ingredients of your compost heap. People? Noise? News? Research? Quiet? Warmth? Chemicals? Size each layer according to the significance it has in your life. Is it a living, breathing, steaming compost heap, or do you have some re-layering and mixing to do?

- Okay, you aren't a gardener, and compost piles aren't your thing. Instead, think about a delicious well-seasoned soup. Plunge your ladle into the stew. What will you come up with? A succulent carrot? A sprig of rosemary? An uncooked bean? Make sure your mind as stew has all the ingredients needed to make a satisfying, fulfilling meal.

- Too many ideas are as dangerous as too few. If your ideas are getting too choked to grow to completion, you have some thinning to do. But take some time to consider: What kind of garden do you want to grow? What will you do with the ideas you don't use right away—stomp on them? Pull them up and return them to the compost? Transplant them? You alone can decide what you need to do.

- It is easy for artists to belittle ideas as they come. "Oh, that one is too small, not deep enough, not serious enough, not what I want at all." Take the time to recognize your ideas— even the smallest, most incomplete ones. Write them down on brightly colored paper. Put them in a beautiful vase. Now pull out an idea. Admire it. Think about it as a seed, as a connection, as a bit of compost. Now light a match, and burn the idea. There is still the ash, right? Like dreams, ideas may change, but they never disappear.

MASK
Fear

. . . .

An empty page. A blank canvas. Silence. Or niggling details. Endless touches to add. Incompletion. Fear is a constant companion during the process of creation. It comes in many forms along the way. There is the fear of beginning; the middle muddle; the fear of ending. Fear can keep you from finding time to do your work, sharing it, or marketing it. Whenever you feel uneasy or doubtful or blocked, fear is whispering in your ear.

Fear takes many shapes. If you are much too busy to do your creative work, that's fear. If family always comes first, that's fear. Perfectionism is fear. So is procrastination.

You have every reason to be terrified. You are treading into areas unknown. You are asking questions that pierce and demanding answers that shake the world.

Fear is a natural response to the artistic process. There are times when fear protects. It stops your work for good reasons. Other times, fear gets in the way of creating. Fortunately, there are ways to recognize the difference and to respond to fear in all its forms. Breathing is one. Holding still and listening is another. Breaking an insur- mountable task into small steps is yet another. Sit with the fear, and you will find that fear is survivable. Doing what is hard to do fills you with courage.

What you will dis- cover as you learn to dance with fear is that a mask may hide, protect, or scare, but behind the mask you are always there, in all your naked exuber- ance, ready to connect.

- Create a mask. When you are done, think about what it means to you. Is this an everyday mask? An artist's mask? A mask that protects? Scares? Hides? When you put it on, do you feel safer? More creative? Silly? You may want to make a series of masks that represents different aspects of your life, or a single mask that consolidates them.

- Make a collage of faces from photos, paintings, magazine ads, sketches. Notice, as you work, that some faces reveal the person within and others act more as barriers. As you go through your next few days, both alone and with others, observe when you wear a mask and when you allow yourself to take it off.

- Make a list of things you fear, both in your work and in your life. Next to each fear, write your natural response. Is it effective? Appropriate? Now write at least three other responses, and evaluate each one as to its probable effectiveness. Choose one fear and one new response, and resolve to act on this fear immediately. This is a good exercise to do regularly, but you really should do it *at least* twice. The first time, pick a not-so-threatening fear/response. The second time, face a creative fear using a new approach. Then ask yourself, "How did it go? What did I learn?"

- Read a scary book. Watch a terrifying movie. Look at a frightening picture. Listen to alarming music. Pay attention to your body's response, your mind's response, your emotions. How are these responses different from and the same as those you have while facing your creative fears?

KNAPSACK
Play

. . . .

There are many ways of setting out on a journey. You can do research, buy maps and guidebooks, hire a house-sitter, pack food and plenty of clothing, and make reservations for each stop along the way. This is a lot of work. You could also just shoulder a knapsack and go. This stone hands you the knapsack—it's time to play.

Who knows what you'll find along your path? Who knows which path to follow? There might not even be a path.

But there will be discoveries to make all along this journey—detours, dead-ends, and delights—and you will find yourself in a world where there are no guides. This is truly the artist's realm, where impossibilities dissolve and new connections are made.

The thought of wandering through such a realm can be frightening. What if you meet blocks as tall as mountains, doubts that take the shape of fierce monsters, or diabolically critical dictators?

Hey! Remember the knapsack? Wherever you go, whatever you meet, it's going to hold what you need. You don't believe? Open it up and look inside. What do you find? Real survival gear—crayon, scissors, glue, glitter, a pennywhistle, balloons, tin foil, and a beanbag frog! What more could you need?

So lighten up. The way into and around this artist's realm is through play. Forget the goal for now, and let go of your time schedule. You are right here, right now. Play!

FOR KNAPSACK, TRY THIS:

- Make yourself a Spontaneity Box. Fill it with stuff that will invite you to play. Make sure you stretch beyond your usual media. Ask friends, acquaintances, and even strangers to add to this "survival knapsack." Then use it.

- Playing is sometimes considered children's work. Observe children at play. Remember games you used to play as a child. Go beyond organized games with rules and expectations into free-flow games, such as jungle, house, blocks. Play them again, either with or without children—not as an adult, but as a kid.

- Look at some of the first work you did. Oh, you're wincing. Really—pull it out, hold it, look it over, listen, watch. There are moments of inspiration, exuberance, new beginnings, hope. Can you still find these in your work?

- Gather together some friends who are artists. Stretch beyond usual borders. If you are a poet, find a potter, a musician, and a dancer. Take turns coming up with playful exercises—perhaps beginner's exercises—in each medium. Those who are experimenting in a new form will be beginners, but even the artist leading the exercise will remember "beginner's mind."

- How often do you allow yourself to play? When all your work is done for the day? Once a week? Okay, get out your calendar. You are going to find one hour this week purely for play, and five minutes every single day during which play will be the work you must do. Schedule it in.

TOOL
Action

. . . .

Paintbrush, fiddle, notebook, clay. Acquiring tools is often our first act of commitment to our art. It gives credence to our desire to be a painter, a musician, a writer, a potter. It reminds us that *being* an artist is contingent upon *doing*.

But there are other tools you need in order to be truly committed: desire, strength, enthusiasm, perseverance, and above all, the ability to take action.

Many would-be artists and even seasoned artists live their days consumed with the idea of a project rather than the actual doing of a project. But today, that has changed. Today you have been blessed with the tools to act.

Choosing a course of action can be difficult. Paths are not always clear. Nevertheless, this rune strongly advises movement. Is there something you're avoiding? Face it. Has a project stalled? Explore it. Most importantly, do not keep that dream (and you know which one) in the planning stages any longer. Begin!

Perhaps you're avoiding the submersion that comes with a plunge into your work. This project will take time and total concentration. With submersion you experience a disconnection from normal daily life. You may even feel as if you'll spend too much time with your art at the expense of others. But, as Kate Hepburn's mother said: "Don't forsake those duties that keep you out of the nuthouse." Know that nurturing your own soul is one of the most necessary and dependable tools for life.

Desire is the potential for creativity. But without action, desire remains intention. With action, desire becomes reality.

FOR TOOL, TRY THIS:

- Imagine or fashion the gatekeeper that's preventing you from taking action. Have a dialogue between the two of you. Negotiate.

- Sometimes our most ambitious projects get pushed aside because they feel overwhelming. We tell ourselves that we need big blocks of time to work on that project—blocks of time that never materialize. So instead of putting the project on hold, break it down into smaller bits. Tell yourself that all you need do today is this one small bit. Begin, and the project will take on momentum.

- Buy yourself the tool for which you've been wishing.

- Complete this sentence: By the end of the week I will...

- Is fear blocking action? If so, go back to the interpretation of the **Fear** rune and try one or two of the accompanying exercises.

WHIRLWIND
Chaos

. . . .

News! Ads! Songs! Weather forecasts! Urgent requests for money! Best-selling books! Movie reviews! Medical breakthroughs! New diets! Latest inventions! Money-saving deals! We are bombarded by information, by exclamations, by noise. Even if we unplug ourselves from the media and surround ourselves only with neighbors and friends, even if we sit alone and listen to the voices in our head, we are exposed to a flood of stimuli. And under all this clamor lies a vast abyss of formless matter, infinite turmoil: Chaos.

Chaos is essential to the artist, for out of chaos comes meaning. Every act of creation begins as the artist finds designs, intentions, and patterns in the disorder. Chaos can also be found in the process of creation, for there are infinite possibilities of order. Again and again, the artist must take a pattern, a fragile concept, a piece of work that threatens to shake apart, and allow it to grow organically until light, life, and meaning suffuse it again.

When you draw this rune, it is time to pay attention to the part chaos plays in your life and your art. Undefinable by nature, chaos cannot be grasped, but its turmoil feeds the soul. Notice what kind of chaos surrounds you. Is it the kind that keeps you from your work, or might it inspire you? If you have shut yourself off from chaos, fearful that you might be overwhelmed by it all, is it time to plunge in? How can chaos enrich you? What patterns can you discover within the chaos that will nourish your creativity?

Chaos can never be tamed, but if you honor it and trust yourself, you'll recognize the patterns you need to discover at this time.

FOR WHIRLWIND, TRY THIS:

- Are you glutted by input? Go on a diet. For the next week, turn off the TV. Don't read the paper. Skip the radio. Don't even reach for a book. The back of cereal boxes? Avert your eyes! Note your reactions. How hooked are you on daily noise? How much are you missing if you don't read the headlines? What other patterns emerge instead?

- Find a newsmagazine or newspaper from ten years ago. Compare it to a news magazine or newspaper from today. How much is different? How much is the same? How much, honestly, is crucial to your life, your work, your art? Based on this knowledge, think how you might adjust the time you spend with external sources of information.

- Go on a walk, searching for patterns. Stop often to examine crystals in rocks, spirals in shells, colors, how leaves are attached to stems or twigs, how insects move. Now find human patterns in bricks and brick walls, building designs, pedestrian rhythms, city street and highway traffic.

- Start a pattern file. It can include pictures, tapes (sound or visual), objects that give you a sense of structure, and notes you make about patterns you find in books, songs, films, dance. Periodically take one item from your file, and see how it might inform a piece on which you are working. Might a dog's yelp give you insight? An Escher print? Drum rhythms? (You might want to start a chaos file, too. What kind of things would you put in that? How much can chaos be contained?)

GAVEL

Judgment

. . . .

Judgment is a necessary part of the creative process. Without it, all choices are equal, and with an infinite number of choices, an artist would be stymied. Which idea to explore? What medium? For whom? Only by judging the relative worth of a possibility can an artist decide how to proceed.

But the judgment many artists know best is stifling. Whether the voice of that critic is on your shoulder, in a rejection letter, or in a terrible review, judgment too often comes down as criticism or censure.

When you draw this rune, it is time to consider the part judgment plays in your work. If you feel that other people have power over your work—the right to tear it apart, negate it, or to

keep you from even beginning—then you need
to explore what else judgment can mean.
Judgment offers you power to compare, to
decide, to understand. By using a healthy dose
of self-criticism, you can discover your own
positive discipline, celebrate strengths in your
work, recognize areas that still challenge you,
and decide how to go about learning what else
you need to know to grow as an artist. Judgment
helps you form your opinions. Being your own
critic, you can decide how you want your work
to proceed and what you want to say.

In masonry, a gavel is used to knock off
rough edges; in law, a gavel raps for attention.
If you allow others
to hold the gavel,
recognize that it
is also yours
to grasp.

For Gavel, Try This:

- Got a critic on your shoulder? More than one? A cacophony of critics? It's time to get to know who they are. Invite them into your consciousness. Give them time to introduce themselves. Get to know their voices, their gestures, their moods. Accept their presence, and listen to their words—not as truth, but as opinion. Often by listening (and they really appreciate it if you write down what they say), you recognize where the voices come from (your second-grade teacher, your critical next-door neighbor, your grandfather). And by opening a dialogue with them, you can negotiate when you want their help and when they need to leave you alone.

- Share a piece you have been working on with a number of friends. (If you are feeling vulnerable, start up a conversation about someone else's work—a movie you've all seen, or a new book.) How many different opinions do you get? Who is right? Do some responses mean more than others? If people have such different reactions to a work of art, how much should their judgments affect your choices? Whose judgment do you value the most?

- How good are you at making choices? Pay attention to the moment you decide something. Go to an ice cream store or a salad bar where many choices are offered. Do you pick familiar items? Do you choose quickly, only to regret later? Are you satisfied with anything? If there is anything you'd like to learn about the power of choosing, practice this exercise regularly.

ARROW
Vulnerability

. . . .

T he artist's soul is perpetually returned to a place of vulnerability. Self-doubt, exposure, envy, personal and professional challenges all stab the very place the artist lays raw in order to create.

How can you recognize and work with your vulnerability? There are many arrows to point the way.

Feeling a lack of validation is one of the most piercing arrows. A desire to give up, to lash out, to turn the work into something it was never intended to be—these are signals that you have traveled too far from your source. Come back to your center. Positive self-opinion is worth an infinite number of accolades.

Hiding your talent or refusing to show your work are surely signs of vulnerability. Instead of risking rejection, you keep yourself clothed. But, like the vain emperor, you are not *really* clothed. You are only parading as safe. Let the **Arrow** rune remind you that genuine safety comes from walking stark naked into the sunshine—the jeering crowd be damned.

Jealousy points to vulnerability—a belief that someone is worthier than you. Jealousy also stems from a belief that the awards, positive reviews, and money are limited in number and therefore out of your reach. Come back to working for the love of working, and you'll find your vulnerability dissipates in your newfound abundance.

Knowledge of self-worth can only come from within.

Embrace vulnerability. It pierces, it prickles, and it smarts. But from your rare, defenseless position comes tremendous growth. Your defenselessness invites perception, truth, independence, wisdom. Being an artist is nothing less than an act of courage. Let yourself be vulnerable.

FOR ARROW, TRY THIS:

- If it doesn't kill you, it makes great art. Find a way to work one terrible, embarrassing, ugly, or boring personal experience into your craft.

- Take time out today to rebuild your strength. Do whatever you need to do to gain a healthy, heartier sense of self. But remember, seeking assurance from others is a Band-Aid without any stickum. Go the journey alone.

- Examine your competitive feelings. Where do they come from? What do they tell you? Does competition serve you well? How?

- Infrequent bouts of insecurity are revealing. Constant feelings of insecurity are debilitating. If you are unable to work due to chronic self-doubt, try removing some of the instigators. Unhappy agent or boasting colleague on the telephone? Don't answer. Unfavorable reviews? Don't read them. Family members refuse to recognize your passion? Don't ask.

- The most powerful remedy for artistic wounds is doing what you love. Get to work.

CLOCK
Organization

. . . .

A t first glance, the pursuit of art may appear
to be rebellion against structure and organization: structured time, structured thinking,
structured modus operandi. However, most
artists soon discover that the act of creating
requires enormous self-discipline (i.e., structure). And, in fact, art itself involves the
creation of meaning—recognizing and teasing
out structure where it was once unrecognized.

This rune is here to remind you that respect-
ing structure will allow you the greatest entry
into making art. Consider first your external
organization, made up of time, your workplace,
your means for collecting ideas and information. Does your external organization honor
your creativity? How often do you show up to

create—not to dabble, not to arrange, but to pour yourself into your work? What prevents you from working more often? When you work, what is the condition of your studio, your study, your corner? Is it a place that supports intense productivity?

Often the first moments of the creative hours are spent organizing. It's easy to justify this time. We say that we must get things in order or we'll never be able to think. And it's true that the very act of organizing does seem to sweep the clutter from our brains as well as out of our work space. But beware, this drive to organize can be one more sabotage in disguise—a form of procrastination. Drawing the **Clock** rune may a be signal that it's time to forget all the preparation and dive right in.

The more you become conscious of your personal needs for structure and of how to support your creativity with organization, the more you will create.

FOR CLOCK, TRY THIS:

- Buy or make yourself a large calendar. Beginning with this month, allow time to organize your creative life, time to work on your art, and time for yourself. When you come to the words *organize, work,* or *me,* do exactly what the calendar says. You have nothing to think about, nothing to negotiate, nothing to feel guilty about. Just follow the directions.

- Look at your body of work. What are the similarities and differences among your pieces? What are the recurring themes? How would you define your collection? Are there structures and patterns you hadn't noticed before? How will they inform your next work?

- Often we keep ourselves somewhere between *really* getting organized and *really* creating. Use this day to reorganize your work space. Tell yourself that under no conditions are you going to work today, you are only going to organize. Then, recharged like a schoolkid with a new pencil box, promise yourself you will keep your workplace sacred.

- Write yourself a list of rules. Begin with, "When I am creating, I..." *may not go to the refrigerator, answer the phone, call my artistic friends, suddenly remember an important errand or bill to pay. I may take deep breaths, light a candle, listen to music, sit and let my mind wander.* Decide how you will reward yourself for following the rules—although the new depth in your work might be reward enough!

- Share your work with other artists. Discuss the work in terms of the organization and/or structure.

X
Failure

· · · ·

The big red X on a page, or the fat F at the
top of it; the review that tears into your
body and rips out your soul; the unfinished
page or canvas; the empty theater; the silent
telephone—all these are signs of failure.

Failure can come from the outside or from
within. It is a dreaded outcome of exposure or
judgment, enough of a reason to freeze. Or it
can be the inability to listen closely enough, to
push deeper, to accept the work you must do.
Failure screams out, "You can't!" and its cries
are so forceful that you believe.

How easy it is to be glib, saying that without
failure there can be no success, that failure
makes us stronger. This may be true, but it
does nothing to take the pain away when the

rejection is utterly overwhelming. Like grief, failure takes its time to loosen its grip. After lessons have been learned and new directions taken, success may color your memories of failure, but it will be your loss if you can't embrace and accept failure itself.

This rune reminds you that failure is a gift. Like a cold or a fruitcake, it is not a gift you can choose; like all gifts, what you do with it is up to you. Think about why failure comes now. What can it tell you? Have you outgrown a mode, a pattern, a way of viewing your work? Don't just think about your failure—wallow in it.

Breathe in failure, accepting it totally. Yes, you failed. Utterly, completely, thoroughly. You can accept it. Failure is part of it all, part of you. Don't *think* about what comes next or even that *anything* comes next. Welcome failure. Hold it...hold it.

For X, Try This:

- Spend twenty minutes to a couple of hours working on a piece, failing intentionally. Write a lousy story; create a thoughtless piece of art. Can you do it? Why or why not? Does it free you? Is it a waste of time? Consider how this work differs from other pieces you have thought to be failures. Think about the benefits and detriments of failure in your creative life.

- Draw a map of your creative life, with crossroads marking choices made by or for you. Take a bright red marker, and circle those moments you have always regarded as failures. Trace the paths you have taken, noting how failure has affected you. Are you satisfied with failure's place in your life? Can you see any patterns? Are there any lessons you are ready to learn now?

- Failure to start; failure to listen; failure to complete; failure to market your work—they all have different causes and need different responses. Can you distinguish between the different failures? Are you in the midst of one now? Which one? Think of one thing you can do to move out of the place where you are. Even the smallest step can move you out of the bog of failure in which you find yourself.

- Make a list of failures that come to mind. For every failure, list a success. Make no comparison of value. Just list both. Now look at your two lists. Think about which—success or failure—figures most powerfully in your life. Do you look at failures and successes proportionately?

EGG
Potential

· · · ·

I magine that the rune in your hand is a hen's egg. Hold it close to your body. Warm it with your breath. Imagine the potential of this egg. Will it be a living, vibrant chick? Will it move, grow, make attachments, thrive? Or is it unfertilized? Is it destined to be scrambled breakfast food?

Now imagine that this egg is your art. What is its potential?

The drawing of this rune signals your readiness to go farther—to bring your art to a fuller, deeper place of creation. Are you working with half a mind, half a heart? If so, how can you dedicate more of yourself? What is standing between you and a more absorbed, intimate, creative process?

Sometimes, to reach your potential, you must give something up. It could be something tangible such as a clean house or preparing a complicated meal every night. It could be something intangible such as a defense mechanism, a "normal" persona ("What would people say if I suddenly produced something irreverent? Something silly? Something with controversial undertones?"), or a destructive belief about yourself. What patterns no longer serve you? What is required for you to work to your fullest potential? Will you allow it?

Sometimes, reaching our potential as artists requires us to reach our potential as whole human beings. Therefore, in order to nurture our art, we must nurture ourselves. This means not denying ourselves the space, the time, the love, the play, the solitude we need. Remember, you have unique gifts. You are here to create. Don't let yourself, or the world, down.

For Egg, Try This:

- Even when we are committed to creating, life's events can get in the way. It is extremely hard to work to our full potential when we're responsible for young children or need to earn a living. If this is your situation, commit on a practice level. Choose your very best twenty minutes of the day and devote them to your art. Make it a ritual, make it sacred. Identify yourself as an artist, and do not give this time up, no matter what. "But I can't make clay, I can't mix paint in twenty minutes," you say. Then sit. And in your mind imagine yourself molding your clay, painting the canvas—see the work, take notes. When you finally do have a stretch of time (and do demand one!), your imagined possibilities can and will become reality.

- Choose one thing that stands between you and going deeper in your art. Give it up.

- Is fear of failure standing between you and your full potential? If so, begin a new piece of work. Now wreck it. Add color from the wrong palette. Change the tempo, add discordant notes. Introduce an unwanted character. Play. Keep working the piece. Let it go wild. How does this feel? Did you learn anything new? You don't have the time? Think of the time you waste holding onto per-fectionistic tendencies.

- Imagine that today you work at your full potential. What happens? What does the day feel like? What does it look like? How does it sound? Write about, paint, compose, sculpt, or dance this day.

[BLANK]
Silence

. . . .

S top...Shush...Be still...Listen. This moment
is asking you to enter into a place of silence.
No sounds, no words, no thoughts...just silence.

Silence. A place seldom visited, and yet
the very place where subterranean meaning,
bewitching imagery, and vibrant, original
connections dwell.

Silence can be entered in several ways. It can
be entered by resting, tool in hand. Close your
eyes, take a deep breath, and release the noise in
your head. As thoughts come back, give them a
nod, then let them go. Remain silent. Longer.
Longer. Longer still. Go deeper. Now you are
in a place of meditation where thoughts, views,
and sounds take an entirely different form.
Swim in the sparkling silence.

Silence can also be entered by taking long, solitary walks (runs, swims, bicycle trips). While you're walking, your mind spins anxieties in one form or another, until all those dos, shoulds, and can'ts are replaced by a quiet listening, and eventually your mind is transported to a place of peaceful, and often joyful, reflection.

One can even enter silence by doing normal tasks with a quiet reverence: washing a dish, sweeping a floor, taking a shower. The key is to stop the mindful bantering and face the moment with an immediate, focused awareness.

Which came first: the artist or the noisy, message-filled, clamoring, compulsively driven art? It doesn't matter. Even if you feel that anger or a relentless message is what drives your work, practice silence. You may discover that your work reaches new, startling levels of communication. For it is in silence that we most often experience the divine.

FOR BLANK, TRY THIS:

- Practice being silent for ten minutes a day. After a week, see if you can increase that time to twenty minutes. Then one day, try remaining silent (without irrelevant noisy head clatter) for a whole hour. Does the practice of silence change your work in any way?

- Take a formal course in meditation.

- Develop a silent prework ritual. Light a candle or heat some scented oil. Hold an object that has special meaning. To quiet your mind, chant or listen to music without lyrics.

- Examine your spiritual beliefs. What is the relationship between your work and the divine? Do your beliefs support growth in your creative work? Would you like to make new connections? How?

- Use silence as a tool against feeling blocked. The next time the right words won't come, the image won't reveal itself, or the notes can't be heard, stop and be silent. Recognize that silence is part of the process. Allow yourself to listen without judgment of any kind. Trust that you will find a way.

MOON
Dream Time

. . . .

Between sleep and wakefulness, there is a landscape where images drift; where connections float together, apart, then together again; where voices chatter, argue, sing, command. This dreamy land offers no permanence, but it can be fruitful when visited on its terms. It is the place of dreams.

Dreams come in many forms: fragments after midnight, drifting day thoughts, sudden visions drenched in clarity, starry glimpses into tomorrow, desperate hopes for the future, night horrors. We can interpret dreams, categorize them, share them, work toward them, or ignore them. Sometimes a vital refuge, dreams occasionally prevent your real work from getting done. Then there are times when the

energy of many people struggling for the real-
ization of a dream ignites whole nations.

When you draw this rune, it is time to
honor your dreams. Listen to them, the ones
that rage and the ones that whisper. Celebrate
the incongruities, the self-glorifying visions.
Welcome nightmares. Be careful not to force
meaning into what must
remain vague and phantas-
magorical, for some dreams
are to be breathed in as a
scent, to flavor our lives and
our work. But if you are
engulfed by a dream that
demands to be
defined, grasp it
and make it
come true.

For Moon, Try This:

- Keep a dream journal. Don't worry about how useful your dreams will be to your work, or that you are forgetting fragments, or that you aren't doing it right. Even jotting a word or two about your dreams in the morning will give many of them back to you. And the ones you lose? They'll go back into the deep to wait until you catch them again.

- If your project could dream, what shape would its dreams take? Artistic creations, like children, may seem to belong to their creators, but they soon develop a place of their own in this world. Can you listen to your project's dreams?

- Visualize how your dreams will come true: the shelf in your office that holds your published work; the scrapbook of newspaper clippings; the opening night of your show. Write a review or a series of reviews about important pieces you dream of completing.

- When you wake from a dream, try to hold an object from that dream in your mind. Now give that object physical life. Build it, paint it, sew it, draw it—and place it on a special shelf or hang it from the ceiling over your bed.

- Are you scheduling enough dream time into your life? If you're not, you'd better start now!

AMULET
Honor

. . . .

As young children, we were naturally drawn to art. We formed—mucking with mud, clay, crayons, or paint. We danced— donning scarves. We composed—full fists on the piano keys. Creating was controlled by feeling, impulse, a quiet voice of knowing. We did not stop to ask: "Is this pleasing to those around us?" We only asked: "Is this pleasing to me?" Art was—and still is—our birthright.

Somewhere along the way, each artist has combined the natural forces of play with the wisdom of experience. Teachers, mentors, masters, and even critics are sought after for lessons and advice. Words such as *technique, practice,* and *form* become mantras. But beware. If the artist isn't careful, the only voices heard are those of the so-called "experts." The internal, intuitive voice is silenced.

The rune of **Honor** reminds you to acknowledge and trust your own instincts. For it is only by honoring what is uniquely yours—your voice, your style, your grace: the wiggle in your step, your bow, your line, or your words—that you can bring to the world something truly original.

Honor your individual work. Listen to your intuition. Wear the amulet of what you know close to your heart.

FOR AMULET, TRY THIS:

- Write ten sentences pertaining to *your* art. Begin each sentence with, "I know..."

- As you work at your craft, strive to be fully present in the moment. Let go of thoughts and concerns pertaining to results. Banish the experts and critiques. Pay attention to how you feel. What does your body tell you? Listen to the inner voice.

- Create a piece of art for your studio that celebrates *you*. What unique qualities does it express?

- Make an amulet. Wear something around your neck that holds a secret. The secret, of course, is what makes your work so wondrous, so powerful.

- How do you know when your work is good—*really good?* Most artists experience a way of knowing. Ask yourself, "What do I need to do now to experience that way of knowing?"

SCALE
Balance

. . . .

C reating is a balancing act. Every moment is
a beginning, demanding both intention
and letting go; production and dream time;
devotion to mind and to heart. Every project
reflects this balance. Some pieces come easily;
others challenge you to develop new skills.
Some may be commissioned; others grow out
of an internal voice. Throughout your life you
will struggle to find a balance between creating
and not creating; between solitude and being
with friends and family; between listening to
voices within and listening to silence.

Balance is never finally achieved, for that
would imply stasis or death. Think of a simple scale. Consider the balance of your work
or working life: thought versus action; sound

versus silence; form versus free flow; work versus play; production versus dreams; inner growth versus family. Balance and lack of balance must come to some equilibrium in your work and life.

The challenge of this rune is not to find *the right balance,* but to explore your needs hiding behind the issues in your life you find out of balance. Each side will have valid points, conflicting points that can never be resolved. Yet in acknowledging and exploring the conflicts, paradoxically, a·working, workable balance can be achieved.

FOR SCALE, TRY THIS:

- Write a dialogue, perhaps using two different-colored pens, between the arguing sides of the balance scale in your work. Listen carefully to capture the voice, the tone, the hidden messages each side is trying to get across.

- Check the balance between the work you do for a living and the work of your heart. It may help if you do this by drawing two pictures: the contents of your brain and the contents of your heart. What takes up too much space? What takes up too little?

- Make yourself a simple balance scale. Use a ruler and a pencil. No. Use a plank and a brick. Better still, head out to a playground and find a teeter-totter. Take some of your work, your tools, or gather a couple of friends and play with balance for a while. Where do you have to sit on the seesaw in order to balance the work you brought? Can you balance your friends and your work?

- Do you know the feeling of balance? One of the best ways to recognize it is to push yourself out of balance. Spend some time working out of balance. Paint a picture, sculpt a figure, create some music, dance, write a piece—something that is purposely off balance, skewed. Pay attention to the energy, the tension that arises in you. Think about when and how you might want to use such unsettled feelings in your work or your life.

- Forget balance today. Do what you really want to do.

TADPOLE
Transformation

· · · ·

One of the major goals of art is transformation: transformation of perception, transformation of thinking, transformation of feeling. Through art, we try to touch the lives of our audience. We want to share something that can change a life—if only for a single, fleeting moment. How can we create art that transforms? By existing, ourselves, in a constant state of transformation.

The beginning artist is most likely to be aware of transformation. Every day brings new learning, new experiments, new growth. Someone learning to create—someone who swims from place to place without the use of land-locked legs—cannot fall back on worn methods or formulaic techniques.

The challenge of the more practiced artist, then, is to maintain a beginner's mind—to come back constantly to a place of unknowing. When facing a blank canvas, the artist must let go of everything he or she has learned thus far. The challenge is to find a new path to the well, a new way of leaping, a new frog to kiss.

Upon drawing this rune, ask yourself, "How am I changing as an artist? Am I seeing, doing, creating differently from the way I did a year ago? How?"

Most artists are a hoppy, restless bunch. We like change. However, sometimes transformation—true transformation—cannot be achieved no matter how much we prod, poke, or push the work. In this case, it might be time to remember that growth is not linear and seldom in our control. Try examining your work for messages, patterns, repeated themes that you may have missed. Give your art the power to transform you once again.

FOR TADPOLE, TRY THIS:

- Draw a time line of your stages of work. On the far left, list your earliest works and what they represented. On the far right, record the work you hope to be doing in the future and why. What do you need to do to work toward your goals?

- Make a visual collage of yourself. Use images from magazines and scraps of materials to represent you. As you work, be aware of what you know about yourself versus what others tell you about yourself. To which voice are you listening? What aspects of your identity have always remained the same? What aspects are new? Celebrate one aspect of personal growth in your work today.

- Keep a creative journal. Before or after you work, take a few minutes to reflect on your creative process—what difficulties you had, what successes you had, what you noticed, what you hope to achieve.

- Say no to that commissioned job that will require you to reproduce past successes. Say yes to trying something new and risky. Leap.

- Find some of your earliest pieces—from when you were six years old, or from when you first began to work in your present medium. Play that simple song on the piano. Read that poem aloud. Find the yellowed picture that hung on the refrigerator. Do you still find freshness, hope, and belief in your work?

CUP
Recharge

. . . .

Coffee break. Spot of tea. Caffeine buzz. Tensies. All over the world, people know the benefits of taking a breather with a cup of some hot drink. There are ritual benefits to boiling the water, infusing the blend, and sitting quietly to sip. Taking a break from a project at hand offers the opportunity for fresh insight or regrouping, perhaps the chance to connect to another person.

When you draw this rune, it is a sign that you need to consider the importance of taking a breather. But before you head off to bring fresh water to a boil, pause to consider what kind of a break you really need. Have you been huddled in a windowless studio for weeks, losing track of the human race? Are you dawdling over lifeless words, passionless colors, empty sounds? Have you been on whirlwind tours, with no time to mull your thoughts or intentions? Make sure you design a break that will truly refresh. And if this is your fifth coffee break today, you may need to bind yourself to your chair and not get up until you have com- pleted an adequate amount of work.

FOR CUP, TRY THIS:

- If you are going to break for coffee or tea, be conscious about it. Turn your preparations into a ritual with intentional steps. Does doing this make a difference in how you return to your work?

- Get out your calendar. Is it full of appointments? Does it register your deadlines? Now get out a pen that writes in your favorite color ink. Go through your calendar, and write in an appointment for yourself every day. Twenty minutes per day is fine most days of the week, but think about a two-hour break on one of the days. And for some time during the year, schedule in a real vacation. Use indelible ink!

- Do you know how to tell whether you need a break or not? The moment you think it is time to pause, stop. You'll know when it's time to choose between a break and sticking with it to get over that hump.

- Go fly a kite! Or jump in the lake! Start a wish list of recharge activities. Keep the list in an obvious place near your work area, and refer to it when you know you need a break—and then follow through!

- Flowers, insects, mammals—many living creatures follow rhythms through each day and night. Humans have shifted from circadian rhythms to schedules of convenience and productivity. Take some time, and design your perfect day. Choose a portion of that perfect day, and discover a way to fit it into your real-life schedule.

LENS
Revision

. . . .

As artists, we take ideas that fill our minds
with images, relationships, emotions, and
do our best to clothe them with sounds, matter,
or movement. It can be an impossible task,
because ideas are ephemeral and not readily
transferable into substance.

Our first attempt to clothe our ideas may
come in a passionate rush or a plodding struggle. It may feel perfect, as if it were meant to be;
or it may be a hard-wrung task that only in the
end has come to take its proper form. Whatever
the character of that first attempt, when it is
finished you have every right to breathe freely,
to shake free and celebrate.

But this rune reminds you that after some
time you need to look again at what you have

created, not in the frenzied state of creative
activity, but in a hushed state. What have you
said? How well have you clothed your original,
wispy idea? If it has changed, did it evolve, or
did you forget? Were the losses worth the gains
in the choices that you made? When is it time
to stop fiddling with the piece, to send it off
and let it become part of the world?

Only you will know the answers to these
questions. This is not to say that others can't
help you. By telling you what they see, hear,
notice about your piece, others may help you
recognize how much of your
work is still in your mind,
and how much has been
translated into matter
or movement.

Although returning
to your creation is
called "revision," the
easiest way to find the
original spark is to quiet your mind
and passively listen. Let your internal
voice lead the way.

- Take some time to look at the world through a lens. Same world, right? But it sure looks different through a Fresnel lens or the wrong end of a pair of binoculars. How can this experience affect your work?

- How much time do you need before you are ready to revise? How can you cleanse your palette of the blinding colors of your work? How will you get the perspective you need? These are not simple questions, and they don't have simple answers, but they are questions you must ask yourself. You can also ask others not for answers, but for opinions. Be aware of your choices and how they can affect the revision process.

- If you decide to share your piece to get some perspective, *STOP*. Think about what you want: Someone to love it? Someone to offer an "objective" point of view? Someone who will fix it? Someone who will reflect your own opinions? Someone who will trash it and remind you of how hopeless you are? Someone who will clearly reflect what she or he sees? Make a list of people you might want to look at your work. Next to each name, list what information you suspect that person can give you. This way, you'll be making a conscious decision about what opinions you'll get.

- Can you make a clear statement about your work? In one sentence, say what your piece is about. Of course you'll miss vital nuances, but if you can't put your whole piece into one sentence, chances are good that you don't know what you're trying to say, and no one else will either.

RIBBON
Celebration

. . . .

I t is difficult for an artist to acknowledge success, for creating is made up of a zillion incremental steps, each one carrying the power to exult or mollify. A beginning artist might establish the moment a piece has been bought as the day to celebrate. But what about the day he or she discovered the voice of the work, tried a new technique, or learned that it's possible to start all over again?

Seasoned artists know that a sale is not always a "happily ever after" experience. There are still conditions to negotiate, revisions to make, people to satisfy. Sometimes the work is dropped unexpectedly. Other times the work is not well received. We begin to believe that celebration will surely jinx a project.

On the contrary. This rune is here to remind
you that you are on an artistic journey—reasons
to be proud are around every corner. Celebrate!
Do not measure the size of the accomplishment.
Don't think of all of the possible events that
could impinge upon your glory. Celebrate.
Celebrate every single moment of triumph.

If you have drawn the rune of **Celebration,**
you have something to commemorate. Take a
moment to reflect on your recent successes.
Then dance, run barefoot, sing a
loud song, write a "hooray
for me" poem.
Send yourself
flowers. Take
yourself out.
Hang a ribbon
in your studio.
Rejoice.

The artistic life is
rich with satisfying,
delectable moments.
Savor every one.

For Ribbon, Try This:

- Hang a celebration poster in your work space. Record each and every moment worthy of celebration. Or begin a celebration chain. Braid new ribbons into the chain to mark moments of success.

- Write down all the actual and possible events that could make you feel successful in your craft. Put an "i" next to those events you listed that are entirely in your control. Put an "o" next to those events that are to some extent out of your control. Examine the outcome. How much of your artistic satisfaction is intrinsic? How much is dependent upon external forces? What does the balance say to you?

- You are probably aware of your external goals (sales, awards), but what about your more immediate, personal goals? What do you hope to achieve today? Write down these goals. Then celebrate your accomplishments.

- How do you celebrate? Do you choose ways that honor yourself, or do you choose ways that secretly undermine what you have gained? Examine your choices. Now treat yourself in a way that shows respect for—rather than challenges—your worth.

- Start a collection of celebration rituals. Dip into many cultures, ask for ideas from friends, think back to how people were honored when you were a child. Practice these rituals. Often. For yourself and for other artists you know. If you don't celebrate something weekly, you are neglecting a human need.

GATE
Marketing

. . . .

Most artists require an audience.
Sometimes acknowledgment of your
work by a friend or family member is enough.
But most artists dream of reaching a larger
audience. And to reach that audience, one
must go to market.

Networking, auditions, samples, submissions—you may
find these words invigorating. In this case, the
Marketing rune is telling you that the time is
right to do what you love. Pick up the phone
and call an old contact. Take your portfolio
around. Send letters to three prospective
buyers. Focus on results.

Unless...you have been too focused on the
market. What are the signs? You're working
entirely on commission. You're creating the

same "successful" style of work over and over again. You're scheduling work years in advance. Although money may be coming in, your art is heading for emotional and creative bankruptcy. Try closing the public gate and stretching your creative mind.

But what if words like *contract, agent,* or *proposal* strike fear at the very core of your heart? Sending or demonstrating work for acceptance can be incredibly daunting. If the work is not received well, confidence falters, creativity gets blocked. Summon the strength from your artistic self and take steps. Build a gate through the wall that separates you from the vendors, the agents, the directors. Each con-tact you make is a prospective partnership. Go to market. Send your work sailing over the gate. Then detach. Let go. Freeing your energy around the work that you sent out will give it more power, giving you the power to keep on creating.

FOR GATE, TRY THIS:

- Too often, all hope is placed on acceptance of our work. Instead, take five minutes each day to visualize the finished product. If you are a writer or illustrator, rather than dream about the call from an editor, in your mind see the finished book. If you are a sculptor, a potter, a painter, rather than dream about the call from the gallery owner or the museum curator, visualize your show. If you are an actor or dancer, go past the hope of a callback and imagine your opening number.

- Make a plan. Determine your market goals. Write them down. Now record all the incremental steps that are necessary to reach that goal. Place a deadline date beside each step. Reward yourself for taking the risks to make your goals reality.

- Take a few moments to ask yourself: "Who is my audience?" Then come up with two or three totally unique ways to present your work to that audience.

- Money is an important part of marketing. Often the more money you make, the more time and freedom you have to devote to your art. Keep a money journal. Decide how much money you want to make this year, and write that figure down. Examine your beliefs about money in relation to your art. Do you believe that all artists must starve? Do you believe that you are deserving of abundance? Why or why not? Determine how you want to think about money and how your beliefs will change your marketing strategy.

More Messages *from the* Muse

. . . .

After using these stones from the muse for a while, you may want to create your own runes using a different medium. Beach stones, clay, Popsicle sticks, bottle caps, bones—many items can become runes. Take some time to decide on an appropriate material. It should be pleasing to your fingers. It should be lasting. And each one should be alike enough so that your busy and directive mind isn't deciding by feel which one to choose.

You may also discover that there are other aspects of your creative process you wish to address. In this case, you'll need to add runes to the bag and words to the commentary. Deciding on a symbol for each new rune and writing the commentary will help you explore that aspect of your creativity. During the process, you will probably find satisfaction in some discoveries you make and find questions you still need to explore. The exercises you develop (or gather from other artists) can lead you toward more answers and, of course, more questions.

There is a danger in writing commentaries. As you write, you will find your thoughts going in an immediate direction, a natural direction, what must surely be the right and only direction. Welcome these first inclinations. They tell you where you are now—vital information. But to move deeper into your work—your creativity—you need to hold yourself still and listen for other possibilities. Word webs, snatches from songs, glimpsed images—all may lead you into places you have yet to explore. Catch as many of these "half-baked" ideas as you can, and see how they might fit into your commentary. Pay attention to the reverse of your rune's meanings (see page 81, "Reversals"). Incorporating the reversals in your commentary can tip your creative world upside down in an instant, and all that blood rushing to your head can be a good thing.

Allow two or three or more interpretations
for each rune. Allow yourself to ask questions.
Permit yourself to leave interpretations open.
But be sure that you work the commentary
until there is a sense of completion. The commentary must be open-ended, but the writing
itself must feel done—at least until you are
ready to make revisions.

Now that we've said all this, remember:
These are *your* runes for *your* creative process.
Directions for the creative journey are yours
for the asking. So ask, then listen carefully to
your stones from the muse.

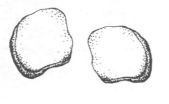

Reversals

. . . .

Whan you draw a stone from the bag and first look at it, the symbol may be upside down. You may choose to ignore this and go directly to the commentary about your chosen symbol. But you may want to consider the implication of the reversal of your rune.

The decision to take a reversal into consideration can be made at any time during your reading, but is most effective when made *before* a stone is drawn from the bag. This way, you will have clarified your intentions before your reading and be less likely to second-guess its meaning. However, there may also be times when you feel something is missing in your meditation on a particular rune or pattern of runes. At times like these, it may be helpful to consider whether the rune you drew was reversed, and if so, how that fact might add to your interpretation.

Reversals are not negative. They do not point to the opposite meaning of each rune. (Therefore, if you draw **Play** from the bag and it is reversed, you don't have to stop exploring immediately and set to "work.") Indeed, some stones are vertically symmetrical and have no reversal. And most of the commentaries we offer incorporate possible interpretations that include opposing meanings.

Instead, reversals offer the opportunity to consider deeper, less conscious reverberations of your message from the muse. There are a number of ways one can tap into these deeper meanings.

A reversed symbol can suggest that you need to look at the negative space surrounding your work as it relates to the stone you draw. After reading the commentary and considering what it means to you, step back. What is not included in your interpretation? What is left out, and why? Your first reaction might be "Everything else." Yet as you move from the overwhelming general to a few specifics, you will discover concepts, meanings, and connections that hover near the edges, waiting to emerge.

For example, you might draw **Organization** reversed. After considering the commentary, you might confidently acknowledge the inherent structure in your work and get back to it. But wait. Because **Organization** was reversed, you pause to consider the structure a little while longer. As you pay attention to the space around your interpretation, you realize that, yes, there is a structure to your work, but it is outmoded. It's time to reshape your work in a more meaningful direction.

It helps to make a physical map of both your initial and your reversal interpretations. Write or draw your initial interpretations, and draw a circle around them. Then add the emergent concepts in the space outside the circle, and see how they take on meaning.

A reversal can also point to a block in your creative work or life. Perhaps you've lost track of your direction or have no idea how to continue. It helps to consider the upside-down symbol as a message from behind your block, showing where you are really going, what you need to aim for.

Often a reversal helps you see an aspect of your work or creative life that you are neglecting, ignoring, or refusing to accept. If you draw **Celebration** reversed from your bag of stones, perhaps you will come to discover that you are neglecting to celebrate some of your smaller successes because you are waiting for "Success" with a capital S. Or perhaps you celebrate only because other people tell you to or will celebrate with you. **Celebration** reversed reminds you to accept responsibility for your own work, your own life.

You may choose not to acknowledge reversals at first or every time you draw a stone, but they can add a new dimension to the messages from your muse.

Combinations

. . . .

O nce you are practiced at reading single rune interpretations, you may want to explore rune combinations.

Milk is milk. An egg is an egg. But egg and milk together become something quite different—eggnog (or an omelet or cake). Reading runes in combination is similar to combining cooking ingredients—each item brings its own essence and yet becomes altered in the mixing. The parts interact to become a new whole.

There are many ways to enter into "combination thinking." Here are a few suggestions.

Draw two runes and place them side by side. Ask yourself questions that lead to new thinking about the influence of one rune upon another. For instance, you might draw **Mask: Fear** and **Knapsack: Play**. Ask yourself, "How does play affect fear?" Possible answers might be:

- *I can't relax for fear that I'll never get back into my work.*
- *I can face my fears in a playful way.*
- *When I play, I tell myself that it's good for my art, but deep down I'm afraid I'm kidding myself.*
- *Play is exactly what I need to chip away at the edges of my fear.*

In what ways does fear have an impact on play? Possible answers:

- *Fear blocks the way to my playful self.*
- *If I'm feeling fearful, it's time to play.*
- *Fear causes me to choose "productive activities" rather than activities that have no purpose other than spontaneous play.*
- *I'm afraid that I've forgotten how to play.*

You might want to play with images to arrive at the combination meaning. Imagine the two rune symbols juxtaposed. For instance, imagine the **Mask** hiding inside the **Knapsack**, or the **Mask** thrown off and the **Knapsack** on your back. What does the relationship of these symbols say to you?

If the symbols are not images you are inclined to work with, give the runes your own visual form. Imagining a gavel with an x may not open visual paths. But perhaps for you, **Judgment** is your pinched third-grade teacher in a tweed suit and heavy oxford shoes. Perhaps **Fear** is falling off a cliff. Put your teacher on the edge of the cliff. What happens?

Try seeing, hearing, dancing a combination of runes. What would a chord that combines **Dream Time** and **Potential** sound like? Can you imagine an **Honor/Action** sculpture?

No doubt, creating a representation of a
rune relationship will enlighten your under-
standing of a combination and of what action
you are meant to take.

As much as we sometimes dream of being
the recluse artist, most of our decisions are
made in the context of a relationship. By
looking at the relationships of runes, you may
be able to recognize personal and artistic
dynamics previously hidden.

The combination meaning is highly personal,
and the possibilities are as diverse as
the people who use this book.
Trust your ability to hear
the combination that is
right for you.

About *the* Authors

. . . .

E mily has been picking up stones since she
was a child. She played with mica, dug gar-
nets out of cliffs, and picked up wishing stones
on the beach. But it's in her artistic life that
she's been finding the real gems—her stones
from the muse. Emily is a teacher, a mountain
climber, and the author of *Hubnuckles* and *The
Missing Fossil Mystery*.

J ennifer has been searching for her muse all
her life. She wasn't able to find it in flute
lessons or chorus ("You must have a cold today,"
said her instructor), in ballet, ballroom, or
modern dance class (though she still dances in
her dreams). Who would have thought that one
day she'd find her muse in a rock? Jennifer is a
freelance writer and the author of *A Net of Stars*.

Notes

. . . .

Notes

. . . .

Notes

. . . .

Notes

. . . .

Notes
. . . .

Notes

· · · ·

Notes

. . . .